APOLOGETICS

APOLOGETICS

The Truth, The Whole Truth, And Nothing But The Truth

Greg L. Bahnsen

The following primer on presuppositional apologetics in the tradition of Cornelius Van Til was adapted from an oral presentation offered by Dr. Greg Bahnsen during an informal debate with Dr. R.C. Sproul in 1977 at the Reformed Theological Seminary in Jackson, Mississippi. See the appendix for more information about the author and the exchange.

A digitally remastered recording of the debate is available as a free download from the Bahnsen Institute. Visit *bahnseninstitute.com* or use the QR code to proceed directly to the relevant page.

Apologetics: Considered Negatively

As we think about the task of Christian apologetics (and the presuppositional method in particular), it might be helpful first to clear the way a bit by explaining what apologetics *is not*.

First, *apologetics is not mere persuasion*. Much of the popular literature in the area of theistic and anti-theistic apologetics consists of highly polemical and emotional efforts at converting others.

To be sure, it is often our duty to seek to convert an opponent to our position. These efforts, however, too frequently substitute mere attempts at psychological persuasion for careful and fair argumentation. Both believers and unbelievers stand guilty in this regard.

Unfortunately, arguments based on poor logic can often prove psychologically effective in convincing people of the truth of a particular position. Conversely, sound arguments can sometimes prove ineffective. Consequently, we may find ourselves confronted by a moral dilemma when we discover that certain bad arguments and glib slogans will be found more convincing by a larger audience than what, in fact, really are *good* arguments.

When, on top of this, we judge the issue that is being disputed to be one of high importance in our lives — such as is the case with apologetics — we are especially tempted to put forth these bad arguments in the service of the truth.

The Christian apologist ought to be the one person on earth who will resist this temptation. We only dishonor the truth — and ultimately dishonor the Lord of truth — when we use fraudulent and specious forms of argument in promoting the truth.

We may persuade a lot of people to become Christians on the basis of very bad arguments, when in reality our task as apologists is to find good arguments that will not be exposed later as fraudulent when someone with greater intellectual talent comes along and exposes our fallacies.

Secondly, *apologetics does not deal in mere probabilities*. We have been called to give a reasoned defense of the *conviction*, or the hope that is in us according to 1 Peter 3:15. When we base our thinking on the apostolic word, we can know assuredly (*asphalōs*, Acts 2:36), and without any doubt whatsoever, that God has made Jesus both Lord and Christ.

This is because the gospel comes to us that we "may have certainty concerning the things [we] have been taught" (Luke 1:4). "Our gospel came to you not only in word, but also in power and in the Holy Spirit and with full conviction" (1 Thessalonians 1:5). The Greek word there (*plērophoria*) means full conviction, assurance, certainty (i.e., perfect faith, not marred by any doubts whatsoever).

The Bible also speaks of our "full assurance of understanding" (Colossians 2:2) and our "full assurance of hope" (Hebrews 6:11). Abraham is called the father of the faithful and, with respect to his faith, Paul says that he "did not weaken in faith," but was "fully convinced" with respect to God's word of promise (Romans 4:19, 21) and thus, the epistle to the Hebrews invites us to draw near unto God "with a true heart in full assurance of faith" and also urges us to "hold fast the confession of our hope without wavering" (10:22–23).

In Christ, we surpass all human probabilities and have bold access to God through confident faith (cf. Paul's prayer in Ephesians 3:14–19). So while the confidence of the godless is as flimsy as a spider's web (Job 8:14), there is, in the fear of the Lord, strong confidence (Proverbs 14:26).

The reason the Proverbs can assert this is because the fear of the Lord is the beginning of all knowledge (1:7). We who put our confidence in Jehovah may "know the certainty of the words of truth" (cf. 22:21, ASV) and thus, I maintain that it is wrong to think that certainty in epistemological matters is limited to formal logic and mathematics.

Certainty (i.e., full certainty, full confidence, without doubt, without yielding, without qualification) pertains to the matters of the Christian faith.

John's emphatic purpose in writing his first

epistle was that his readers might have confident knowledge of their salvation. Therefore, the *Westminster Confession of Faith* teaches us that believers "may, in this life, be certainly assured that they are in the state of grace" (18.1) and continues to make very clear its meaning when it says, "This certainty is not a bare conjectural and probable persuasion grounded upon a fallible hope; but an infallible assurance of faith founded upon the divine truth" (18.2).

Apologetics, then, is a discipline that deals with the hope that is in us (i.e., with demonstrations that yield full conviction). Apologetics does not deal in mere probabilities, but in "the full assurance of faith" (Hebrews 10:22).

As a brief aside, talk of "moral persuasion" or "moral certainty" at this point is simply a cop-out. For whatever that strange state of mind is supposed to be, it is not compatible with mere rational probability. Moral assurance is to be based on the apprehended strength of the evidence and, as all philosophers who have spoken of this suspicious state of mind have said, it is to be proportioned to the certainty of the evidence itself.

Apologetics is not mere persuasion, and it also does not deal in mere probabilities. It is important to underscore this point. We are not simply trying to persuade people. We are interested in the true grounds for our Christian faith. We are not talking about what is *probably* true, but rather what is fully and unyieldingly true.

Apologetics: Considered Positively

The Apostle Paul asks in 1 Corinthians 1:20, "Where is the one who is wise? Where is the scribe? Where is the debater of this age? Has not God made foolish the wisdom of the world?" In that one phrase, we find the battle cry of presuppositional apologetics: "Has not God made foolish the wisdom of the world (age)?"

Our apologetical procedure is twofold according to Proverbs 26:4–5. It is how we show the foolishness of the wisdom of this age:

> **Answer not a fool according to his folly,**
> **lest you be like him yourself.**
> **Answer a fool according to his folly,**
> **lest he be wise in his own eyes.**

The Proverb first says, "Answer not a fool according to his folly, lest you be like him yourself." That is, do not answer a fool according to *his* approach to things, or according to his folly, or according to his assumptions or presuppositions (if I can import that term). You are not to answer it that way, because then you are going to be like him. You will be like an enemy behind the lines.

Yet the Proverb continues, "Answer a fool according to his folly." This, by the way, is not a violation of the law of contradiction. Instead, it is simply setting forth a twofold procedure for defending the faith.

First, *don't* answer an opponent according to his folly, lest you fall into the same pit with him. Then, *do* answer him according to his folly. Why? "Lest he be wise in his own conceits."

You must show the unbeliever that he has no ground for his conceited knowledge. You must show him that God has made foolish the wisdom of this age.

Paul says in Colossians 2:3 that "in Christ are hidden all the treasures of wisdom and knowledge."

Yes, all the treasures of wisdom and knowledge (be they pertaining to logic, or to causality, or to natural science, or morality, or whatsoever)!

All knowledge is deposited in Christ and thus Paul is able to say that since all the treasures of wisdom and knowledge are in Christ, you should see to it that no one "robs you" through what he calls "vain philosophy and empty deception" (paraphrasing vs. 8). Paul describes "vain" philosophy in terms of thinking that is "according to the traditions of men" (i.e., according to the elementary principles of worldly learning, *rather than* according to Christ).

The presuppositional model of apologetics instructs us not to answer a fool according to his elementary principles of learning, because we will become like him. Instead, we are called to answer according to *our own* presuppositions — those that are according to Christ — for then we will be able to conclude with Paul that "God made foolish the wisdom of this world."

The nature of the apologetical situation can be stated briefly in this way: First, the controversy between the believer and the unbeliever is *in principle* an antithesis between two complete systems of thought, involving ultimate commitments and ultimate assumptions.

Second, even the laws of thought and the laws of methodology, along with one's factual evidence, will be accepted and evaluated in light of those governing presuppositions.

Third, all chains of argumentation (especially over matters of ultimate personal importance) will trace back to, and will depend on, starting points which are taken as self-evident. Thus, *circularity* in debate will be *unavoidable*. That is not, however, to say that all circles are intelligible or valid.

Fourth, and because this is the case, appeals to logic, appeals to fact, and appeals to personality may be necessary in apologetics, but they are never apologetically adequate. What is needed are not piecemeal replies, probabilities, or isolated evidences, but rather an attack upon the underlying presuppositions of the unbeliever's entire system of thought.

Finally, and according to Scripture, the unbeliever's system of thought can be characterized as follows:

By nature, every unbeliever bears the image of God (cf. Genesis 1:26–27), and is therefore *inescapably religious*. His heart testifies continually to him, as does also the clear revelation of God around him, that God exists, and that he has a certain character.

Further, the unbeliever exchanges the truth of God for a lie (cf. Romans. 1:18–25). He is therefore a fool who refuses to begin his thinking with reverence for the Lord. He will not build on Christ's self-evidencing words. He will instead suppress the unavoidable revelation of God in nature.

Because the unbeliever delights not in understanding but chooses to serve the creature rather than the Creator, he is self-confidently committed to his own ways of thought; being convinced that it is not possible that he might be fundamentally wrong. The unbeliever flaunts perverse thinking and challenges the self-attesting Word of God.

Consequently, the unbeliever's thinking results in ignorance. In his darkened, futile mind, he actually hates knowledge and can gain only a "knowledge falsely so-called," as Paul says in 1 Timothy 6:20 (ASV).

To the extent that he actually knows anything, it is due to his unacknowledged dependence upon suppressed truth — the suppressed truth of God within him. This renders the unbeliever *intellectually schizophrenic*. Because of his espoused way of thinking, he is actually opposing himself, and showing the need for a radical change of mind so that he might gain a genuine knowledge of the truth.

Nonetheless, the unbeliever's ignorance is still a *culpable* ignorance, He is "without excuse" for his rebellion against God's self-revelation (Romans 1:20) and he is (literally) "without an apologetic" (i.e., without a defense for his thoughts).

The unbelief of the non-Christian does not stem from a lack of actual evidence, but from his refusal to submit to the authoritative Word of God from the very beginning of his thinking.

Apologetics: God's Requirement

Having considered the intellectual situation into which we are thrust as "defenders" of the faith, it is necessary that we now consider the question, "What are the requirements of us as apologists?"

First of all, I would say that the apologist must have a proper *attitude*. He cannot be arrogant or quarrelsome. He must, with humility and respect ("meekness and fear" per 1 Peter 3:15), set forth his arguments in a gentle and peaceable fashion.

Second, the apologist must have the proper *starting point*. He must take God's Word as his self-evidencing presupposition. He must think God's thoughts after him, rather than attempting to be neutral in his debate. He must view God's Word as more sure than even his personal experience of the facts.

Third, the apologist must adopt a proper *method*. Working on the unbeliever's unacknowledged presuppositions, and being firmly grounded in his own presuppositions, the apologists must aim to cast down every high imagination that is exalted against the knowledge of God by aiming to bring every thought — his own as well as his opponent's — captive to the obedience of Christ (cf. 2 Corinthians 10:5).

Fourth, the apologist must have the proper *goal*. His aim is to secure the unbeliever's unconditional surrender, without compromising his own fidelity to the Word of God.

The "word of the cross" must be used to expose the pseudo-wisdom of the world as destructive foolishness (1 Corinthians 1:18–19), and Christ must be set apart as Lord in one's heart (1 Peter 3:15), thus acknowledging no higher authority than God's Word, and refusing to suspend our intellectual commitment to the truth of that Word.

Apologetics: The Method

In light of the intellectual situation and these requirements for the apologist, let us finally consider what should be our procedure for defending the faith.

First, realizing that the unbeliever is "holding back the truth in unrighteousness," the apologist should *reject* the foolish presuppositions implicit in his opponent's critical questions and assertions, and instead attempt to educate him.

This will involve presenting the facts within the context of the biblical philosophy of fact. Notice we *do* present the facts — we are "evidentialists" — but we present them within a presuppositional framework where they make sense.

That framework is this: That God is the

sovereign determiner of all possibility and impossibility. A proper reception and understanding of the facts will require submission to the Lordship of Christ.

The facts will be significant to the unbeliever only if he has a presuppositional change of mind — from darkness to light — and Scripture alone has authority to declare what has happened in history, and to interpret what has happened.

Scripture not only declares the fact that Jesus rose from the dead (e.g., 1 Corinthians 15:3–4), but that he did so to secure our justification (Romans 4:25).

Next, the unbeliever's espoused presuppositions must be forcefully attacked. He needs to be asked whether knowledge is even possible given his espoused presuppositions. We must *demonstrate* that God has made foolish the wisdom of the world.

The believer should place himself, as it were, in the unbeliever's intellectual position, and proceed to "answer him according to his folly, lest he be wise in his own conceits." That is, we can demonstrate the outcome of unbelieving thought based on its own assumptions.

The unbeliever's claim should be reduced to impotence and impossibility by an internal critique of his system. We must demonstrate the ignorance of unbelief by arguing from the impossibility of anything contrary to Christianity.

During this dismantling, the apologist should be sure to appeal to the unbeliever as a true bearer of the image of God who has the clear and inescapable revelation of God available to him, thus giving him an ineradicable knowledge of his Creator.

This knowledge can often be exposed by indicating unwitting expressions in the unbeliever or by pointing to the "borrowed capital" (i.e., the unadmitted presuppositions that cannot be found in his philosophical system).

Finally, the apologist should declare the self-evidencing and authoritative truth of God as the precondition of all intelligibility and man's only way of salvation from all of the effects of sin, be they ignorance or intellectual vanity.

Lest the apologist become like the unbeliever,

he should not answer him according to his folly but according to God's Word.

The unbeliever should be invited to put himself on the Christian's intellectual foundation, in order to see that it alone provides the necessary grounds for intelligible experience and factual knowledge, thereby concluding that it alone is truly reasonable, and that it provides the very foundation for proving anything whatsoever.

Further, the apologist must show that Scripture accounts for the unbeliever's own state of mind — his hostility to God's truth and his refusal to acknowledge the necessary truth of God's revelation.

Scripture alone provides the only escape from the effects of this hostility and failure, be they intellectual futility or eternal damnation.

Apologetics: No Compromise

In conclusion, we must not compromise the faith in order to defend the faith. The Bible gives us an entire ontology (what is real), epistemology (how we can know), and ethic (how we should live).

In defending the faith, it is essential that we do justice to the Bible's whole teaching on the level of our apologetic presuppositions, as well as our apologetic methodology.

Our goal is not simply to defend an abstract system of thought, but ultimately — in the power of the Holy Spirit — to *persuade* men (2 Corinthians 5:11), and that persuasion comes from a faithful presentation of the truth, the whole truth, and nothing but the truth.

The Bahnsen Institute exists to introduce a new generation of Christians to the work of the late Greg L. Bahnsen (1948–1995).

Dr. Bahnsen was a theologian, apologist, and ethicist whose ministry spanned the last quarter of the 20th Century. He received his theological training at Westminster Theological Seminary in Philadelphia, PA, and was granted his PhD in philosophy from the University of Southern California. Working within the Reformed theological tradition, he was a student and proponent of the "presuppositional" apologetic method pioneered by Cornelius Van Til.

His more academic books (*Theonomy in Christian Ethics* and *Van Til's Apologetic: Readings and Analysis*) are considered definitive in their fields by many, but more often than not, his writings — many of them published following his untimely death from complications of open-heart surgery in 1995 — are aimed at a popular audience.

Books such as *Always Ready: Directions for Defending the Faith*, *Presuppositional Apologetics: Stated and Defended*, and *Homosexuality: A Biblical View* have been of immense value to individual believers interested in thinking God's thoughts after him and living a consistently biblical ethical life.

Bahnsen was a minister in the Orthodox Presbyterian Church with years of pastoral and discipleship experience. He was always concerned to add the principles and methods of presuppositional apologetics — developed in the academic study — to the "toolbox" of every believer that was interested in giving a reason for the hope he or she has (cf. 1 Peter 3:15).

Accordingly, he was regularly found "taking it to the streets" (in the words of the popular song); holding conferences and seminars that were accessible to a wide range of Christians across the country and the globe. This little book is offered to the Christian public with that same desire.

Bahnsen was also interested to take the apologetic fight to the enemies of biblical faith — the proponents of naturalism, agnosticism, atheism, humanism, and those who practice the "ethics" of lawlessness. He was a bold and effective debater, and was willing to take on anyone who would engage.

As his reputation grew (especially after his debate with noted atheist Gordon Stein), the willingness of opponents to meet his challenges chilled considerably. In fact, one noted atheist even withdrew from an already-scheduled and advertised debate with Bahnsen.

Not only were these debates models for the deployment of presuppositional apologetic arguments, but God used them to embolden many Christians who had been intimidated by the bluster of the village atheist.

Thankfully, especially in view of Bahnsen's early death, much of his oral ministry at conferences, debates, seminars, and sermons has been preserved with audio recordings, which have been remastered and are available under the auspices of the Bahnsen Institute.

In the American evangelical world, "everything is debatable" and apologetical principles and methods are no exception. Even within the smaller world of "Reformed" theology and apologetics, the discussions between those who espouse the so-called "classical" model and "presuppositionalists" have been ongoing and oftentimes heated.

One of the most able and popular proponents of the "classical" approach was the late R.C. Sproul, founder and director of Ligonier Ministries.

In 1977, an exchange was arranged at Reformed Theological Seminary in Jackson, Mississippi between Dr. Sproul and Dr. Bahnsen, who was at the time a member of the faculty at the seminary. It is often referred to as a "debate," but it was more an informal, and extremely cordial, exchange of views between the two apologists.

Both men stressed the many theological assumptions they shared as heart-committed Reformed ministers. Further, the two agreed as to the goal of apologetics (i.e., to both defend the faith and persuade men).

Each offered a presentation, and the floor was then opened to the small audience of seminary students present (there were no formal rebuttals or questioning between the men).

The Bahnsen Institute shares Dr. Bahnsen's personal burden to equip all the saints for the work of ministry in the propagation and defense of the faith once delivered to the church by the Spirit of the risen Lord Jesus in the pages of Holy Scripture. May this little volume be of help to the reader to that end.

An audio recording of the full exchange is available through the Bahnsen Institute. Visit their website at *bahnseninstitute.com* or use the QR code.

Roger Wagner
January, 2024